To Kelly,

Infinite Sequels

POEMS BY
David Stones

May all your sequels
be infinite !

Best,

David Stones

Oct. 19/20

Produced by:

FriesenPress
Suite 300 – 852 Fort Street
Victoria, BC, Canada V8W 1H8

www.friesenpress.com

Distributed to the trade by The Ingram Book Company

Table of Contents

For Mum & Dad

And particularly for Jeannie
who supports and shapes my vision
and lets me be me

ALMOST

I was almost something, I almost began
I almost got started, changed flesh into man

Almost a poet, stitching words from wine
the dark balladeer in search of a rhyme

So nearly a judge, commanding the case
almost an actor, except for this face

Almost in commerce, trading lies for success
almost a saviour for those who confess

A life full of joy, a life in grief
a life of abundance, a life too brief

Almost mistaken and partially right
half in the shadows, so close to the light

Small in your coldness, so swollen in heat
close to uplifted, nearly complete

Almost a husband, almost a man
the chains of my being, anchored in sand

So lost in my darkness, so radiant in grace
I'm just killin' time, tryin' to find my place

Almost a lover, almost a friend
almost a beginning, almost an end

I was almost something, I almost began
I almost got started, changed flesh into man.

PRAYER

Let me change what I can change
Let me undo what I can undo
Let me arrange what I must arrange
Let me renew what I can renew

Let me sing what I can sing
Let what was true be once again true
Let me begin what I am chosen to begin
Let me praise the broken, bless the few

Let me unbraid the right from the wrong
Let me provide what's needed and due
Let me find the words to the song
Let me refuse what must be refused

There is a balance, a sense of perfection
It's exact, it's precise and it's pure
Let me know the purpose, the aim and direction
Let me endure what I am made to endure

Let me change what I can change
Let me reveal what others obscure
Let me arrange what I must arrange
Let me endure what I am made to endure

David Stones

EMILY DICKINSON

I have this recurring dream
where D.H. Lawrence
and Ernest Hemingway
pin Emily Dickinson
to the floor
while Sylvia Plath
tickles her without mercy.

I don't know why
these particular authors
are involved
or what any of this means.

But afterward
in the dream
Emily Dickinson writes a poem
about a tree
and then another one
about a spider
that spins a web
from the earth to the moon.

In another dream
in another dream that I have sometimes
Emily Dickinson and Sylvia Plath
lie in each other's arms
just staring at that web
suspended across the night sky
like a trellis of tears
silvered and wet with love
in the darkness.

THE POET

In this summer silence
hermetically still as time bleeds
across the sprinklered lawns

is my whole life shining
charged and fused
with its wick of burning flesh.

I knew it then
before the bleached wires of sun
how a life in art
spiders its dark stain
into the grey hard rocks

into the trailing hearts
we chase
but never catch.

David Stones

INTO THE LACQUERED AIR OF EVENING

Into the lacquered air of evening
the birds issue their sharp beaks
to dress into song
the closing flowers.

All around the little park
I hear the windows slowly breathing
their final gulp of sun.

Just another day of beauty
shutting down
before the hunched and grovelling poet
assigned the verdict
to somehow bring about
the gauze of promise
we'll call tomorrow.

BLACK BOX

You taught how love can best be hoarded
how the heart can best be thwarted
They're gonna find
that black box in our wreckage
and let us know
what failed.

You taught that feelings must be sorted
how the fuse is best aborted
Well the bombs
are in the envelopes baby
and the letters
have been mailed.

There is truth and what's purported
what's decried and what's applauded
Sometime's love
is seeking harbour
when the heart's
already sailed.

There's the lie and what's reported
what's abandoned and what's supported
We slash
the face of beauty
but the scars
have all been veiled.

Love is ridiculed love is lauded
it's lost but it's all recorded
They're gonna find
that black box in our wreckage
and let us know
what failed.

-London, 2010

David Stones

HAIKU FOR BLUE HERON

alert blue needle

weighs the possibilities

rigid with silence

-Consecon, 2009

ALL WILL REJOIN

Branches dissect
and ribbon the wind
but the wind rejoins
its willowing hands
to belly the spinnaker
and polish the land.

Islands pierce and divide
the river's strands
but the river rejoins
its waters embrace
the curtain once torn
is returned to lace.

I watch a flame
how it flutters and breaks
but the flame rejoins
remains pure and whole
consuming our hearts
consuming our souls.

Every particle that passes
will segment in the end
but all will rejoin
will become seamless again
the hearts and the rivers
the strangers and friends

all will rejoin
become seamless again.

David Stones

A HIGHER PURPOSE

I have been informed
that I am intended
for a higher purpose.

As no one
yet has
told me
what that
might be

I just
go about
my breathing

watching for signals

alert to instructions
from unlikely sources.

ENDING

he abandoned then
the very shape of him

floating down

an umbrella parted
to the demands of flesh
the denial of bone
against the purpled bruise
of skin

such a meagre dropping petal

I watched him fall
until his sentence
rouged the pavement
in a Rorschach stain
not he or any of his disciples
would ever understand

STACCATO

Woman thinks her life is like staccato, hard piercing, rough
edges, sharp, rhythmic needles of longing. Nothing is con-
tinuous, no conclusions, chains of starting and stopping, exits,
entrances, vignettes. Woman carries her pain, weeps often. I
need anchors, links, things to hold me, a cradle for my heart.

Cat watches with smoky boredom. Cat perceives, objectifies, weeps
with woman. Or does not. Just cat on bed watching woman weep,
cat detached, only able to relate to own pain, own desires.

Woman strokes cat. Cat yields slow murmur, rolls head under
caressing fingers. Cat adores attention. Woman identifies
with cat, weeps more, imprints the torn flag of her soul.

Grace of cat is constant. Cat is constant. Woman holds cat close.
Woman smiles, embraces cat. Cat is many things. Many things cat
is not. Cat is not staccato. Cat hears woman's heart, beating.

AS CRUCIFIED AS I

I met another Poet
as crucified as I
I've written all your poems before He said
to which I asked Him why

He said I saw you rising like a sun
your words diffused by light
you may be the prophet but I'm the One
to tell the stories in the night

I used your words to create a path
for what was and is to be
each poem a beacon and a stone
once the lock and now the key

I thanked the Poet and kissed His robe
thanked Him for sky and star and birds
said thanks for measuring out my life
of love and light and words

David Stones

CRAVING

The deserted mall
a dream while waking
the abandoned call
a wave not breaking

A leaning wall
the wound not aching
the darkened hall
to love while hating

A gloveless hand
an empty room
the ship unmanned
a quarter moon

A keyless grand
a silent loon
the child unplanned
the barren womb

I DID IT

I did it.

Dredged
from the ruin
of my anguish
and desiccation
yet another
cherished fucking bloom
we're permitted
to anoint
a poem
in accordance
with the celestial rules
of artistic endeavour
and our failed attempts
in the great
human exercise.

To which
my wife would say
why fucking
why tarnish the rose
with your sickness?

To which I say
it connotes
the struggle, my love,
to order the collisions
of all these spinning fucking words
that command a shape
despite my slight
and sloping form
humbled
before my passage
through the daunting
fucking archway
of invention.

David Stones

IT ISN'T POETRY

It isn't poetry
to just fasten
sadness to the page

like this

SILENCE ISN'T SILENCE ANYMORE

Silence isn't silence anymore.

I hear it now
singing and spitting its hot breath
across the coils
pushing itself into spaces
obdurate and invasive
as the moon.

Silence makes noises now.

At night
it freights the darkness
with its lolling tongue
teasing my eyelids
with incantations
telling me it loves me
when I know it doesn't.

Silence
is a poor
and lying lover.

Beside me
it does not move.

Its blackness hisses lies.

Resolute and spurned
it regards the ceiling.

Coiled and waiting
I hear it
urging me
to speak.

David Stones

PARK AT DUSK

in
lengthening
custard
bruises
the sun
tie-dyes
the grass

before the butterflies
and the babies
on parade

-The Little Park, 2012

OLD GUITAR STRINGS

The strings scarred and spent
I release them
from their moorings

tired, played out
falling like clipped curls
on the flowered rug

they just lie there
songs cut loose
a pile of severed words

pointless beginnings
forgotten endings
for the cat to play in
as the final step
in their humiliation.

There will be fresh songs.

There will be more music.

The new strings gleam
with promise
and obedience.

But the old strings
they have nothing to say now.

They just lie there
a pile of dead ends
used hearts
in the heap of weightless serenades
we come to know
as yesterday.

David Stones

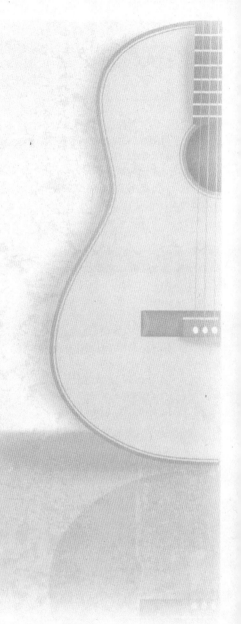

MY GUITAR JUST IS

Every guitar eventually weeps.

Lennon, Lorca, Cohen...

is there a poet living
who hasn't etched those words
at some point
in their miserable life?

Well mine has never wept.

It sobs.

It sobs
because I
bring neither weeping to its soul
or extract it
from the cedary
perfumed pit
of its being.

Neither giving or receiving
neither weeping or believing

my
guitar
just
is.

EACH IN ITS PLACE

The sunflowers
dial their dusty heads
just one way
to catch the truest light.

Before the cabanas
and the casinos
precise and punctual
as escalator steps
the waves
unwind their dark folds.

Birdsong commands
the leaves to stillness.

In this congruency
I believe again
in the dizzying hairs
of love

my faith deepened
in the vast possibility
of forgiveness
for all things.

THIS CHRISTMAS NIGHT

This Christmas night
the cruel red mouth
of the OPEN sign
at the massage parlour door
humbles our revolution.

It is the wound.

Behind the blankets
deployed as shields
at the window sockets
we watch the shadows
circle and embrace.

Thus on this holiest of nights
are we given
a new definition of loneliness.

We have the wound
and now the knife
turning.

THE IDOLS

Every night
you have to smash
the idols

you can start
with the car
in the driveway
then move to the mirrors
even include the kids
if you have to

the objective
is purity of purpose
the cleansing of being

pared down
you'll stand
straw-thin
the genital warts
staring back
like planets

you can kiss
the surface
of the pond now

but there's no prince there
to charm the tumult
into stillness

the idols are gone
and the frog's
gonna stay a frog

forever

David Stones

THE NAMELESS ONE

"And your name?"

"I have no name."

"I must have a name. I cannot proceed without a name. Without
a name there is no victim. And without the persecuted there is
no story. The action is obviated, without cause or effect."

He surveyed the room. In his hand he balanced the symmetry
of a crystal elephant. Through the glistening vault of its girth his
hand was magnified, a planet swollen in the truth of its orbit.

"But I have no name."

It was all I knew. It was all I was authorized to say.
I was not permitted to speak more words.

"Then you understand your path?"

"I do."

My voice came from another voice. My truth came from a deeper truth.

He called me nameless one
and walked upon my grave
he played my song and surfed upon
the mercy of my wave.

He said I was the nameless one
and that this made me brave
without a voice, devoid of words
in my silence I was saved.

I PUT ROY ORBISON ON

I put Roy Orbison on

I remember that much

I put Roy Orbison on
because I needed to feel
despairing and without purpose
and Orbison
could always
take me there
particularly in those
flat bleached days
when you whacked
all the meaning
out of me

all that day
I watched the door
that you
walked through
I became the empty ashtray
the orange
in the bowl
the object waiting
for utility

but the door
remained closed

congealed
might be
a better term
congealed shut
with mean and clotted words

the shape of you gone
with the click click

of your stiletto heels
on the wooden floor
of that little flat
where first I traced
the sighing breathless highways
of your flesh

all day
that door retained
its shape

through Crying and Pretty
Woman
held fast
keeping the world out
and the trembling in

only as the room darkened
and frailty latticed the walls
did I know
the day was done

and yet
that door
remained
as closed
as any door
could be

your clothes
bloodless
as crucifixions
spiked
to the shadows

David Stones

UNDER THIS RETREATING SUN

Under this retreating sun
from bricks sweating
their gold and ancient butter
the buildings fret their stories
into the evening air.

In the local pool
the woman is a solitary figure
a narrative singular
in its innocence
a lone rose
pulsing.

She alone indents the gathering night
accepting with each assertion
of her glistening head
the dark and rhythmic weight
of history
and a fragment
of the day to come.

THE ORDER

The order was given
the instruction was clear
execute her at dawn
drown the bitch in her tears

We gathered beforehand
with a gun and a spade
we spoke of her kisses
we spoke of her grave

One rouged her lips
another braided her hair
we selected the dress
for her death to wear

Forgive us we said
the barrel black as a cave
but the gun on her brain
took as much as it gave

I remember a moment
between time and despair
when her hair in my hands
was as weightless as air

When her eyes held the starlight
and the truth on her lips
exploded in smoke
under my fingertips

Yes there once was a moment
when the world seemed so new
when we were driven by love
and what we had to do

David Stones

SNOW

snow
punctures
an already wilting
sky
weights silence
to the ground

I'm wearing
the wrong shoes
for the occasion

I slither and slide
towards an embrace
I calculate
may occur by Thursday
somewhere
in the Western World

that last shot
of Balvenie
still corrodes
gnaws like white noise
at my ego's
flimsy hinge

I'm reduced
my friend

come and get me
snow plastered
and trolling
for a premise
on streets
I fail to identify

my context
for the evening
is you

and the hurt
you unfold
like a burnt flag
over the defeated grave
of our marriage bed

the snow is solitary
but not silent
there is the piercing
of the white-stained green

another bar
sirens its smashed lipstick
stare
into the torment

perhaps
that embrace
is there
or at least
a face
a face
I might find useful
in my campaign
to challenge darkness
or just to contain
within my meagre
nest of hands

I try to bum
a cigarette
and hum a little prayer

let me love again
before I die
and let Thursday
come
before Thursday

EVERYTHING

The music wounds me
with long soft darts
My eyes moisten
with surprised tears
Everything is suspended
in this light
weak with winter

I fill this space
completely now
The orchids arc
a chain of bruises
bowed by
their own stillness

Beyond the cat
sleeping on the sill
beyond the glass
beyond everything
motionless and ordered
within this room
clings one last rubied leaf
to the tree outside
waving
like a child's hand

David Stones

I JUST WANT TO LOVE YOU

I tried smoking cigarettes.

But the ash was too pale
The smoke was too blue
My dreams were too frail
To stand up to you.

I thought fingers of scotch might do the trick.

But the nose was too sweet
With its toffee and spice
I can't love you neat
I can't stand you with ice.

I tried all the drugs I could find on the street.

But most made me placid
Some made me berserk
With some I was flaccid
With most just absurd.

You see I just want to love you.

There must be a narcotic
That guards against hurt
And I'll search 'til I've got it
The potion that works.

PAINKILLER

Pain..........killer

Curious word that.

I don't know
of any other noun
that we kill
so unceremoniously.

But it's a fascinating word
captivating even.

Pain..........killer

I could stare at it all day.
I think I will.
I'll stare at it all day
stare it down.

In my spine
the sun is setting.
White embers
of explicit something
but I can't say what.

Hills and trees
are famously eliminated
from the landscape.

I could walk
for hours now.

I think I will.

I'll walk for hours
out this door
along this featureless dial
the clock face

with its hands gone
where I move
with such
effortless dignity.

David Stones

SHE STOOD IN THE LIGHT

She stood in the light
and nothing seemed right
just the truth of the moon
on her face.
And we might try again
but I can't say when
and I can't give the
time or the place.

So we walked on the beach
with her soul out of reach
and my heart drifting
over the sea.
And I look at the sky
and I have to ask why
why there's a riddle
called me.

We met in a spring
infused with lemon and gin
her perfume put the flowers
to shame.
And then came the night
it shattered the light
it frightened the moth
from the flame.

Sometimes it seems
life pierces our dreams
and we're left where the waves
drum the shore.
But the moon will give way
to the birds and the day
of this, my love
I am sure.

Of this, my love
I am sure.

-Lyrics to a song, 2007

FRAGRANCE WILL DO

I don't want to be deep
I want to be perfect.

I don't seek complexity
just to be understood.

I don't need my words twisted
just braided into beauty.

I don't need a lover
fragrance will do.

I don't need absolution
my sins are unique.

I don't need the darkness
for I bend to the light.

I won't worship the many
but I'll bless the few.

I don't need a lover
fragrance will do.

David Stones

ALL NIGHT

All night
the percussive knock
of sea boats
on the dark green wall.

All night
the wind aching
from the blackened rocks
across this glistening bay of tears.

All night
a stillness in the watery tombs
that hide the pounding
of the freezing waves
beneath the cold hard moon.

All night
the sea birds
pulsing warm and full of dreams
amid the swaying pines
before the rage of frightened
secrets
locked and burning still
within the sifting vaults
within the stories
and the ruined hearts
the leading and supporting parts
the empty glass
the finished wine
the brimming soul
the dying vine
the dust
the bliss
the wound

the kiss
all night
    the world
        will turn
            like this.

-Carter's Beach, Nova Scotia, 2009

HAIKU FOR A GOOD BAR

good bars are old wood

worn smooth with truth and caring

infused with regret

David Stones

INEXORABLE

I cleaned the fence
almost reverently
just to have that foul raccoon
plod back
and shit on it all over again
impervious to the tenderness
of my endeavour
and efforts
to rid the world
of his horror.

This is how the hours
illuminate the clock
preventing anything from stopping
even when we sleep.

Jets trail
their vapour
in frayed ropes
across a night sky
while the windows
glow like pilot lights
and the raccoon
lumbers its fat ass into place
for another glorious crap.

THANK YOU

thank you
for listening

but I wasn't
talking to you

David Stones

HOW IT HAPPENS

This is how it happens. I can only make this pronouncement
once so allow it to command your complete attention. Do not be
disturbed by how the clouds shrapnel into frayed flesh or the way
the sunlight poisons the snow from the blackened branches.

Brothers and sisters, fasten on the picture. It happens only once.
Stationary camera freezes the street, the vague lens of hills, the
parabola of insolence we call committal. The world obeys because for
such things are the laws made. It is all very beautiful, this forming,
this shaping of all the loose ends. In the acquiescence, the breath of
poppies explodes in compressed knuckles of perfume and starlight.

Enter frame right. On a tricycle a small boy pedals against the
will of nightfall. Frame becomes monochromatic. Bare trees sway
skeletal and bloodless in a sepia landscape. Boy proceeds through
frame. Stops. Stares down camera's discerning eye. There is the
anxious sting of his passage. If he could, he would stay, right there,
suspended mid-frame in perfect triangulated balance, perpetual in
his youth, his song ascending. He reverses. Circles. Boy exits frame
left. Off frame his cry. Jubilant. Defeated. Constrained. Released.
The poppies announce themselves, escaping the monochrome with
minor stabs of colour and mechanical nods before a sinking sun.

This is how it happens, friends. The events have to go down like this.

If there is any other order, any deviation from this sequence,
then what has happened did not happen, and these words
carved into the page to prophesy and lie will no longer exist.

OUR MOMENT

The sun descending
    the mirrored water
the swans endless
    in their silence

Everything glowing
    serenely suspended
ready for our moment
    to walk naked
into the vast garden
    of creation

David Stones

THE POEM JUST MELTED

The poem
just melted

its meaning lost
to firmer resolutions
and higher grades
of prophecy.

My hands remain
wet with its words
a spare veneer
of meaning
that speaks of love
and all the things
that matter
before the bleeding
before the letting
of the language
from our wounds.

I'm sorry
I doubted you, love.

I'm sorry
I held our poem
so close its heart bled out.

Just give me
another fragment,
my sweet

one more
fragrant little piece.

I'll hold it close again
I promise that

but not so tight
as to dissolve
the burning fuse
of its purpose.

EARLY ONE WINTER'S MORNING

The bus took her out
early one winter's morning
a right hand turn
the witness said
a turn of fate
a right hand twist
in the early morning
with the snow just starting
and her day laid out
packaged and perfect
like her lunch
in the little satchel
prepared with love
love for herself
and love for others
before that last sad step
from morning into night
when the bus put an end to everything
but the snow
coming down
and her lunch
left just
lying there

David Stones

CLICHÉ

Though one man's cliché
is another man's rainbow

the hackneyed phrase
is the poet's poison

and must be avoided
at all costs.

FROM ALL THAT SHE SAID

From all that she said
I got the impression
that she did not care for love
she'd played before
and did not like the rules
or the end result.

But when she laid her dress
over the chair
I caught it up
and stretched it tight
like skin across her face
to kiss her
through the damp cotton.

I don't why I did it.
It just seemed right
for the moment.

She lay imprisoned
like a butterfly
pegged to the earth
with silver pins
the dress wet
with our hunger.

I retreated from the moment
as I sometimes did
in those broken days
and it was only then
that I saw her damaged wings
and I realized why
she did not care for love
and how lonely escape must be
when you do not know
what you are leaving.

I disentangled the dress
and gathered her in

and she has become my lover
and my tired starling.

-Toronto, 1971

David Stones

THE SCENE IS ALL JAZZ

The scene is all jazz
full of louses and lushes
they're all workin' the room
the drummer the brushes

A palpable longing
is both near yet remote
from the crowd pierce her eyes
shards of turquoise in smoke

She rubs against me
her openness raw and at play
it's so wondrous, so healing
to be used in this way

She says you're lovely, you're a jewel
her voice lifting and free
and I would have left with her
if she was talkin' to me

WHERE POEMS END

He could no longer
decipher
where his poems
were supposed
to end

how to whittle
the little sticks
of language
into the sculptured
cul-de-sacs of closure
we need to urge
the image
from the stone.

In time
he grew
less troubled
by these
severed filaments
left dangling
from the open coils
of his imagination

devoting his time
instead
to the larger issue
of determining
where his poems
were required
to begin.

David Stones

IN CERTAIN LIGHT

In certain light
we see the source of the pain
In certain light
we're sure where to aim
In certain light
we call beauty by name
The light refracts true
is first the candle
then the flame

In certain light
we're a byte of memory a byte of
dross
In certain light
we offer wine before the cross
In certain light
there's the win and the loss
The light refracts true
is first the crevice
then the moss

It's just some daylight
then some night in refrain
it's just a pathway along the river
where we came
it's okay to be alone in the game
it's okay to walk again
the pathway where we came

In certain light
we're just a number on a street
In certain light
we can only retreat
In certain light
we find victory in defeat
The light refracts true
is first the ember
then the heat

In certain light
we're better apart
In certain light
we see the end not the start
In certain light
we see the will not the heart
The light refracts true
is first the bull's eye
then the dart

It's just some daylight
then some night in refrain
it's just a pathway along the river
where we came
it's okay to be alone in the game
it's okay to walk again
the pathway where we came

PER JEANNIE IN TOSCANO

I no longer write the poems.

When silence veins
the milky hills
and your flesh is still

you become my music
and my wine
and the poems write me.

-Firenze, Toscano, 2011

David Stones

INTO THE MORNING

into the morning
the flowers explode
their bright and bursting throats

weeping
would go well here

the ambience is perfect
for anything wounded

or even this pathetic
withered prick

and by that
I mean the person
not the body part
though the latter too
could use a little
attentive coaxing
from an understanding soul
who understands the immutable splendour
of a summer garden
and the elusive balance
of love

YOU AS LACUNA

Your awayness
has become a presence now
a space
you've somehow filled with space
your shape on the bed
still rosy with your fragrance.

Filling the house
the clock ticks
the only moving thing
resolute
as a pallbearer's boots.

In the afternoon
clouds roll in
before cold fists of rain
staccato the windows.

On the flowered bedspread
the cat finds
your shallow grave
to inhale your sleep
rhythmic as the rain.

Even the cat's breathing
is audible
on this day
as time passes
on schedule
and without consequence.

David Stones

IF THERE WAS

If there was
some kind of symmetry
a linked knot
a one-to-one relational
string theory
of words and stars
you'd think that I would have
discovered it by now.

If there was
a way
to slot these tumblers
into the exact ordained sequence
to make them dance
with just the right
degree of stirring
and delight
you'd think by now
I'd have that
pretty well nailed.

Well I don't.
It's not nailed at all.

Hence the nights
becoming day
the flowers despairing
by the garden fence
as I grapple
with yet another page of
white
white
white
laughing.

PAYMENT

You pay the woman
you pay the man
to become the rock
so you can remain
the water

David Stones

THE ENORMITY OF BEING

I'm not sure
what kind of tree that is
I can't tell you
that woman's name
that breed of dog eludes me
what I don't know
I can't retain.

That bird is speckled
but I don't know the species
the blossoms are flaming
but must go unnamed
and this person looks vaguely familiar
I'd say hello
but discreetly refrain.

The curve of her hip
is perfectly exquisite
but the angle
I can't really say
her eyes are the colour of something
but it escapes me
and just drifts away.

This park is alive
and soaking with questions
with propositions
and options anew
but the depths of my ignorance are infinite
answers are scarce
and conclusions too few.

THE TIME WILL COME

The time will come when I can no longer order the words on the page as I am pretending to do here. Not even senseless words chained to their inconsequence and the raw drip of their meaning.

At this purpled hour my love for you will deepen its irreverent stain into the eager blotter of your beauty. You will hold my hand in that tidy reverential fold you save for the generous moments. We will think of the beach and the boardwalk and the night we swallowed the moon in our happiness. Again we see the lake ignite with the punctures of a thousand stars. Your skin becomes the rivers and the meadows of my breathing.

Into your round harbour I curl as a child, your voice a hypodermic piercing my flesh with my own words.

David Stones

SEQUENCE

He dreams.
She dreams.
They meet.
They dream.

She dreams.
He dreams.
They meet.
They dream.

They dream.
He dreams.
She dreams.
They meet.

They all work
one way or another.

But I've tried
that last one
and it's
not so good.

Best to dream together.

Best to let
your dreams
temper who you are
and who
you might become.

MY VOICE

Once again
my voice has let me down.

All my life
I've been a man
of good intentions
sure and healing hands
a lifted heart.

But always lurks
the cruel joke
of the tattered tongue
the mouth
that mocks me
with a bruising smile
of its own.

Maybe in some other life
I'll be allowed
to just rap on
in liberated
liquid speech
while on the hills
in the ruby blood
of autumn
the crowds gather
just to touch my robe
before the honeyed altar
of my phrases.

· David Stones

THE SWEET MACHINE

we weep
more freely
when the healing
is complete

yet another irony
of the sweet machine
that is the human heart

SOME WENT OFF IN SHIPS

Some went off in ships

some exhorted the heavens

some consulted the Holy Books
until they were exhausted
with adoration

some prayed with the old men

some knew too much

some knew too little

some said no to death
so their brothers could shudder
in their hard cocoons of darkness

let me love you love

let me know your loveliness
until the harbour
fills with ships
and there is light again
to gild the rooftops
and welcome
the sailors home

SPRING

steady

sure
about
everything

hawk
rides
ribbons
of wind
above
the steaming
furrows

UMBRELLAS

You try
different hotels.

Are you
the keys
or the tumblers?
It no longer matters.

To understand the ending
you need to know
how it begins.

What is the alpha?
What is the omega?

You just want
everything to be okay again.
It has to all
fall into place.

But it's
not going to.

By the time
you get the room
it's already too late.

You stand at the window
diminished as the rain
watching the people
manoeuvre the wet street
under their umbrellas.

David Stones

HOW TO CATCH MICE

the best way
to catch mice
is to bait the trap twice
but not to set it

the third night
you strike

the little bastard dies
with a brittle snap
the body weightless
as a bird's
bones full of air
straws hollow
as subways

you hear it
in the darkness

the verification
of your wisdom

your refusal
to accept defeat
from a fucking little rodent
several thousand times less
than your body weight

WHAT AM I

What am I
but air
just some eyebrows
on the wind
a bit of flesh and hair
on whose soul
some hopes are pinned

What am I
but sand
just grains
before the sun
I'm slain before I started
before the blindfold
and the gun

David Stones

THE LILT AND BEND OF SHAPES

This Macallan 18 commands worship of a higher enterprise. I have boarded an abandoned street car of embrace and goodbye. But I like it here and the waitress is beginning to sound like bells. Outside the fog has taken the air away. Birds drip and sag from the wet wires. The harbour has surrendered to the lilt and bend of shapes.

This place is almost empty now save the couple by the window toiling in the vast embroidery of love. On the table she places her small, white hands. And for too long they lie there, frightened and alone against the dark wood. And then over them he places his own, captures in his own the small, white, frightened loaves of her hands and raises them to his lips. And she watches his face and she says yes, yes, this is what I wanted, yes....Such are the small mercies enacted in Port Mouton before the dripping robins.

Our lady of the bells pays a visit and asks well what have we learned today. And that is when I write this down, my lifetime of accumulated knowledge tempered by Mr. Macallan and all the poems that have leaked out of me for almost 60 years. That love retreats from sorrow and sorrow from the rags of love. That the line upon the page is the only truth, though words can result in darkness. And too often, too often it is the human heart that fails against the grey folds of rain.

-Port Mouton, 2009

WORDS

The sky
is parchment
crowded with symbols
the words
and the songs
of our journey.

The language
of the night
hangs heavy brother.
It titters
anxious and malevolent
above me
on my veins
its nervous pressing.

Words can ache
and weep
like old wounds
some kind
some evil
some cruel
some merciful.

I fear this night.

I fear what the sky
can do
with its huge
unknowing eye.

I fear
the weight of language
and intent
that hones the tumbling
alphabet of stars
against the humbled presence
of my being.

David Stones

TWO STONES

With the patience
and exactness
of Stonehenge
my granddaughter
wove into position
the two polished stones
on the larger rock.

What they symbolized
to her
that autumn day
we'll never know.

But in the spring
ordered yet
within the precision
of their
assigned roles

the two stones
still bore the
loving signature
of her small hands.

MY HOLY BOOK

bowed
but not yet
broken
spine fissured
with the brittle pith
of its own wisdom

my Holy Book
still casts its
slender beam
into the chaos

David Stones

YOUR INNER LOVE

Believing in your inner love
I put my faith in you
I did not think the darkening dove
could love you as I do

No rose presented in your prayers
could render you more pure
no song so sweet nor wine so rare
could so conquer and endure

Your form was warm behind the lace
I could feel the honey and the heat
but in the beauty lurks an inner grace
we find the leech beneath the sheet

I loved you for your inner love
I know you loved me too
in time we both embraced the darkening dove
who loved us as I loved you

UPON THIS PAGE

Upon this page
I nail the finite phrases
they imbedded in my brain.

Not even the sweetness
of the summer night
or the sculptured logic
of your face
can free more words
or drive the singing little clusters
we might call poems
we use
to soak up sorrow.

David Stones

ON NIGHTS LIKE THIS

Was it large needles and small thread
or large thread and small needles
that quilt into whole cloth
our daily bleeding
that weld our pieces
into such a soft and heaving fury?

I don't remember.

At dusk
on black and stuttering wings
the bats came out
to argue the guttering heavens.

Small under a rosy sky
we drank more wine
and laughed
toasting our love
for each other.

Perhaps
I think
it is the finest needles
and the most exquisite thread
that stitch such
brimming greedy minutes
to bring us friends like these
on nights like this.

UNTITLED

poems

even the good ones

are sometimes

worth saving

David Stones

IT GETS TO THE POINT

It gets to the point
where you simply cannot
or no longer think you can
even move
or adjust the way
your weight invents the bed
distributes pain
to new-found pockets
of longing.

The fire on your tongue
goes out
and you just lie there
listening to the seawall roll
of your heaviness
the breathless tears of blood
clenching into unthinkable
laughing fists.

No longer can you dream.

You can only look back now.

And this you do.

With a tenderness
searing and lucid
you look back
until your eyes grow heavy with peace
and you are allowed to see
for the first time
that only through this ending
comes the permission
to be born again.

POEM NUMBER 5

My mother lost an eye to cancer
didn't really lose it
just watched it with her other eye
sifting back
a depleted sun
a star spent
in the inverted universe
of her drifting soul.

She loved us all
in different ways.
I know that now.

In the final days
her one good eye
had a shining bewildered love.

I watched it radiate.

In my grief
that one good eye
shone bright as any constellation
straining out to fathom
how a life might end
but love go on forever.

David Stones

THE MIRROR

In increments the snow erases the garden, weighs down the
hedge like a white-haired drooping eyebrow at the edge of the road.
From the window he watches the runnels, the wind stooping the
trees. He imagines how he must look from the street: a reflective
suggestion behind the glass, now glimpsed then lost. He likes this
pose of detachment, the impervious review of chaos. It is the glass
that makes him master, the glass by which he is diminished.

And then he crosses over. Into the jewelled world he takes a
shovel. And there looks back, looks up to see himself at the same
high window. He admires his double, the demeanour and the
studied stance, his quiet way of watching things. He wonders
which the flesh and which the image. As does the double wonder.
Which the blood? Which the matter? Which the bone?

Thus the mirror, it has two sides as does the glass.
Motionless we stand, one at the window, one in the
white, still garden until the snow begins again.

FASTER

Faster
my love implored
please faster
with a whispering sigh.

But my ancient slobbering lover's tongue
so wise and harnessed by splendour
knew best
went slow
made the circles ache
and drove
my heaving breathless angel
to the very brink of heaven.

Later
in my arms
her body turned to smoke
she said
that was the last time
she would ever offer me directions.

And then I combed
the soft and golden round
of her sleeping head
and all her dreams came out
in a drifting easy bruise
of broken stars.

David Stones

EVERY STONE IN TURN

Every stone in turn
and perfected grace
they form a crust
upon this place

This skin we walk
drink the sky above
it makes us whole
it lets us love

It says we can live
says we can die
it allows the truth
permits the lie

WHAT I KNOW

My masters say
that I must write about
what I know the most

That is why
I write about
my love for you

This is what I know
inside out
and upside down

I know its depth
and its breadth
its darkness and light
I know it by stealth
and I know it on sight

I know its flesh
and its touch
its bark and its bite
its pink inner life
and its moan in the night

I know when it speaks
I've wept when it can't
I've cringed at its stutter
and applauded its chant

Love starts
and it stops
like the shreds
of a ghost

It's all
that I know

It's what I know
the most

David Stones

TORONTO ROBINS

Yesterday
I saw a tree
frosted with the
toasted orange
of a dozen robins.

I swear
in January
in Toronto
at least a dozen robins
with their breasts
as warm and bright as marmalade
warbling in the sun.

I don't know
who was right
the weather or the robins.

But all day long
I hugged close
the trembling burning orange
of those dearest birds
and what they let me see

the lift and wonder of their song
and what they gave to me.

THE SUN

The sun warmed my face
this morning
while I raked the yard.

I watched it
divide the clouds
come down in threads
through the branches and wires
to where my face was waiting
tired of winter
a goblet ready for its wine.

I make some notes:

be more gracious to the sun
declare more often
my gratitude for its kindness

remain a vessel waiting
receptive to love
open to blessing

David Stones

SO EXACTLY YOU

You ask
if I saw
you naked.

No,
I lie

believing my evasion
might save you
just a wedge
of what you hold
as your manisfestation
in the eyes
of The Holy One.

In my life
I have melted the bones
of too many convictions
both my own
and those held dear
by others.

No,
I did not
see you naked.

When I left
you turned
to watch me go
but stopped your gaze
before the mirror
startled
to see the image
was so exactly you.

THE NIGHT READY TO RECEIVE ME

The night ready to receive me
The Macallan motionless in its vessel
My hat waiting and patient as a dog
I approach the page
Place on its white slate a woman
Give her eyes pellucid
And empty as corridors
Give her a room and a shape
Write in a stale coffee on the sideboard
Beside the purse with a broken strap
Put her there on the bed
The sheets Rorschached
With their badges of sex
Still moist with the rings
Of their weeping
Scatter around her
The letters, the needles, the 45
And I'm almost done
My job nearly complete
Save the matter of the singing
Save the matter of the song
Save the matter of the words
I'll fasten to the woman's lips
Blackened with outrage
In her last quivering moment
Of breathing
Before the Macallan does me in
And I'm permitted
To look dangerous again
In a rakish fedora
And the woman imbedded
And the night coming on
Neither cold enough for winter
Or warm enough to match
The inspiration
Of this early spring

David Stones

IT DIDN'T MAKE MUCH SENSE

It didn't make much sense
to go on believing
in the revolution
with my skin gone
and my nipples
sucked pale
by the tyranny
of your contrition.

It was more logical
to enter the storm
with my hands bound
my tongue extended
to receive the sleet
and the desiccated wafer
of your confession.

By the tracks
I knelt
and bowed my head
for your sweet anointment.

But there was no blessing
just the 10:26
to Montreal
which gratefully missed me
as I pissed with exquisite aim
into an abandoned
bird's nest
beside the trestle

enacting
I'm sure
a rite of remarkable symbolism
understood only
by diseased poets
and the confused robins

who once made my urinal
their home.

SOLITUDE

the larger
the crowd

the more crimson
the laceration
of my solitude

WITHOUT SUGGESTION

Without suggestion
or notice
the vine withered
from grace

became a phrase
ill-used
in the general lexicon
of mortal certitude.

Our gardener shook his head
grimly
with his diagnosis.

Cardiovascular disease he called it.

It just happens he said
and then he compared it to the
clouds
forming and dissolving
into trailing balloons of vapour
as though that
explained everything.

Well for me it almost did.

It explained life
and it explained death.
It explained love
and it explained loss.

I poured a scotch
just a finger
and I thought hard
about everything.

I thought about what coalesces
and what divides

what punctures
and what heals.

And as the garden
softened into weightless shadow
I thought of veins gone wrong
a heart shut off
by the cold sure valve
of uncertainty.

I ENTERED A KISS

I entered a kiss
there was never a doubt
turned my back on the moon
but I could not get out

I entered a kiss
my heart was true
an entry forever
into the arms of you

I entered a kiss
moist and fragrant throughout
turned my back on the sun
but I could not get out

David Stones

HORSES

horses
before
a setting
sun

caged hopes
and what might
have been

prayers
chained
to the ground
now

fastening
field
to sky

LEAVES

Leaves burn
their shape
into the wet pavement.

Come spring
they'll still be there
dusty shadows of being
scalded into the crust
like nuked bodies
blasted into nothingness.

When I am gone
will your flesh
be branded
with the lovely stain
of who I was
of all I gave
to our singing
vision of immortality?

When I am gone
I hope you see me
always
stamped on your landscape

the very image of me
a part of all your journeys
boundless and pressed
without limit
into your soul.

David Stones

THE TIDES

I forgave the water.

You wept on my shoulder
but I could be
neither rock
nor solace.

Standing on the shore
or walking on the sea
I was devoid
of harbour.

I drank your dew.

Fog swelled
the tender rivers
of my bones.

Listen, my love.

When you are sleeping
I listen for the tides
until the tides
fight back
with stories
of their own.

ON THE BLEAKER DAYS

it is only
on the bleaker days

that she
fathoms
the shapes
forming
and reforming
beyond
the torn
blood curtain
of her eyelids

these are
the days
when nothing
seems
to work

nothing
seems
to make
a difference

these are
the days
when she
cannot imagine
anything
that she
might do
that would
have even
the smallest
repercussion

David Stones

MY FATHER'S MEDALS

My father's medals
are now too heavy
for him to wear.

They weigh down
his small chest
stoop him over
with their long tales
of death and boredom
corned beef for breakfast
and body parts steaming
on the Burmese Front.

My father despises
what happened to him
over there.

He'll tell you that
settled in his chair
by the window
delivering a reflective swirl
to his beloved CC and ginger
as if the glass itself
holds the stories
he feels so compelled to relate.

My father lost a wife
to that war.

He lost his youth
and his innocence
close to sixty pounds
and his very perception
of being.

He gained a few things
as well
I guess.

He learned how to smoke ciga-
rettes
and all about fragility.
He discovered what it means
to treasure
and how distance
intensifies love.

He found out
what's worth fighting for
and what isn't
and not just in terms
of the war.

That's what he'll tell you.

He'll tell you exactly that...

in his chair by the window
rotating his rye
until his medals
tremble on his narrow chest
like leaves
about to fall.

-*Remembrance Day, 2012*

Infinite Sequels

THE SWEET KINDNESS OF BEING

it is the sweet kindness of being
that permits me
to be the only one
in this blistered
lonely place
to assemble these words
in this exact order

such are the options decided
within the arc
of infinite possibility

David Stones

THE OLD DAYS

I remember the old days

pizza from Buzz Buzz
night becoming
a brilliant bandage
in the eastern sky

we spoke of love
and permanence
and all things
resilient to change

as though souls
and inner truth
could somehow
remain impervious
like steely sheets
of glacial rock
hammered into indifference
by a million years of punishment

life proved
not to be like that
at all

it filed us down
inch by inch
like those hard rocks
defeated by rain

I see you now
our granddaughters
fastened on your eyes
like trailing comets
and I think what might have been

if life
was not quite so full of flint

our spirits not so inclined to anger
our memories not so quick
to forget the love and haunt
of Buzz Buzz pizza
double cheese and pepperoni
delivered hot
to Borden Street
on dear careering nights
at 3 a.m.

PUTTING OUT

just like that
it all closes

ball teetering
until it drops
before the severed stalks
frozen in the fields
raw
under a sullen sky

above the greens
nailed to the clouds
geese work the headwind

clamouring and furious
to escape winter

David Stones

OUT OF DEATH (beginnings come)

Out of death
beginnings come.

The day my friend died
I thought
of the first time
I loved

my first
dark bruise
of sorrow

the soft
blue music
of love returned.

And that night
I heard the wind
as never before

polishing the stars
with exquisite
unyielding gifts
of forgiveness.

POEM HITS GLASS

There is
before impact
a silence
turgid as any silence
its edges smoothed
by endings
the dark milk
of tragic possibility.

And then
just a result

the bird stunned
blunted and conspicuous
as a billiard ball.

Does it know
how the words
gather at its side

tumble from its throat
in scarred clusters?

Look at its peering.

Does it understand
how love reflects
soft in hard glass

until this collision
until this ultimate
imperfect melding
with the endless mirrors
of poetry?

David Stones

I'M SORRY

I'm sorry
to be the one
with the soft edges
and the hard reality

but it's deathbed time now
the hour of revelation.

Listen up:

nothing
gets
solved.

Nothing.

ALMOST

I was almost something, I almost began
I almost got started, changed flesh into man

Almost a poet, stitching words from wine
the dark balladeer in search of a rhyme

So nearly a judge, commanding the case
almost an actor, except for this face

Almost in commerce, trading lies for success
almost a saviour for those who confess

A life full of joy, a life in grief
a life of abundance, a life too brief

Almost mistaken and partially right
half in the shadows, so close to the light

Small in your coldness, swollen in heat
close to uplifted, nearly complete

Almost a husband, almost a man
the chains of my being, anchored in sand

So lost in my darkness, so radiant in grace
I'm just killin' time, tryin' to find my place

Almost a lover, almost a friend
almost a beginning, almost an end

I was almost something, I almost began
I almost got started, changed flesh into man.

David Stones

Index of Titles

David Stones

ACKNOWLEDGEMENTS

Building a book like this is done in increments, one brick at a time, one word at a time carefully wrought out and manoeuvred into position.

While most of *Infinite Sequels* was written over the last two years, the build process was really initiated many decades ago when the first seeds of language and a developing love of the poetic voice began to surface as an important part of whom I was and whom I wanted to be.

For this I am indebted to my family, and in particular to my late but fearsomely articulate mother. A cadre of poetry masters, from classicists to moderns, have also had deep impact on the shaping of my craft, particularly Dylan Thomas, e.e. cummings, Irving Layton, D.H. Lawrence, William Butler Yeats, Leonard Cohen, Raymond Souster, Emily Dickinson, Louis MacNiece, W.H. Auden, and the tragically beautiful Sylvia Plath.

I would also be remiss were I to omit the wonderful and calming influence of my dear daughter, Caitlin, likewise a poet of life, and her two extensions of the Creator, Ryan and Zoe. Many of the more embracing, gracious and thankful poems in *Infinite Sequels* are written with them in mind.

I am immensely grateful to Glenn Pound and his company, Launch Communications, for his tireless contribution and powerful use of timely images which elevate and provide depth to some of the pieces. Glenn's input to the cover design was also instrumental, as was the dedication and talents of the Friesen Press team throughout the process.

And finally, I again thank my wonderful wife, Jeannie, who endured first drafts of many of these poems, often spoken late at night as she drifted off to another world. Well, love, I didn't always have a chocolate for your pillow, so I thought I'd just leave the lingering fragrance of a poem instead.....Thanks for listening. There's a lot more to come.

David Stones
June, 2013

Printed in Canada